THE CEASELESS CENTURY

THE CEASELESS CENTURY

300 YEARS OF EIGHTEENTH-CENTURY COSTUME

RICHARD MARTIN

PHOTOGRAPHS BY KARIN L. WILLIS

THE METROPOLITAN MUSEUM OF ART, NEW YORK

This volume has been published in conjunction with the exhibition "The Ceaseless Century: 300 Years of Eighteenth-Century Costume," held at The Metropolitan Museum of Art from September 9, 1998, through November 22, 1998.

Published by The Metropolitan Museum of Art, New York

John P. O'Neill, Editor in Chief
Barbara Cavaliere, Editor
Design by Matsumoto Incorporated, New York

Library of Congress Cataloging-in-Publication Data is available on request.

isbn 0-87099-884-6

The color photography in this volume is by Karin L. Willis, The Photograph Studio, The Metropolitan Museum of Art.

Unless otherwise indicated, all the costumes in this volume are in the collection of The Costume Institute, The Metropolitan Museum of Art. The frontispiece and the illustration at the beginning of each chapter are in the collection of the Irene Lewisohn Costume Reference Library, The Costume Institute.

Color separations by Professional Graphics, Rockford, Illinois
Printed by Julio Soto Impresor, S.A., Madrid
Bound by Encuadernación Ramos, S.A., Madrid
Printing and binding coordinated by Ediciones El Viso, S.A., Madrid

Front cover left: Gianni Versace, *Evening ensemble,* spring-summer 1992. Navy-blue denim, gold and black silk faille with lace. Courtesy Gianni Versace Archives

Versace's eighteenth century was lusty, cinematic, and volcanic, extracted from and exaggerated from Casanova and de Laclos. Versace's passionate history was always in some ways self-justifying, allowing the past to seem a fit predicate for the late twentieth century. In his book *Rock and Royalty* (1996), the eighteenth century and contemporary celebrity are constantly juxtaposed, justifying a kind of Elton John ancien régime. Here, the skirt might pass as a very flirtatious Versailles, but the denim top deliberately fails any historicist dress code.

Front cover right: English. *Mantua and petticoat,* 1690-1695. See pages 22-23.

Frontispiece: Georges Lepepe. Robe du Soir, de Jeanne Lanvin. *Gazette du Bon Ton,* July 1924

Back cover: Olivier Theyskens, *Evening dress,* 1998. Brown and red striped natural vintage recycled linens. Courtesy Olivier Theyskens

Like the rich linens employed and often embroidered in eighteenth-century dress (see pages 36-37 for a prime example), a deconstructed, yet extravagant dress reconsiders both the silhouette and material of eighteenth-century style. Erudite in its historicism, the dress is not less elegiac in its sensibility for a sweeping train in contrast to a corseted and constricted torso and not less compelling as contemporary fashion made, in this instance, by a designer in his twenties. Ramshackle yet resplendent, Theyskens's gown testifies to a distinctly 1990s affinity to the past, one that does not "copy" but conveys and interprets to a new epoch.

CONTENTS

fig. 1

FOREWORD

I remember two great exhibitions of eighteenth-century dress drawn from the collection of The Costume Institute. For many visitors, the most unforgettable was the 1981-82 exhibition "The Eighteenth-Century Woman" (fig. 1), using our collection, but lavishly supplemented with international loans. I have a personal favorite in "Costume: Period Rooms Re-Occupied in Style" (November 27, 1963-January 5, 1964) (fig. 2), an exhibition in which key pieces from The Costume Institute were deployed on mannequins to become revenant inhabitants of those otherwise unoccupied rooms. Perhaps my fond memory of this exhibition is colored by the fact that I had just joined the Department of European Paintings as a curatorial assistant and it was the first costume exhibition during my tenure at The Metropolitan Museum of Art.

In fact, when I first met with Richard Martin to invite him to become Curator of The Costume Institute, I thought I would tantalize him with this splendid and unrepeated opportunity. I suggested that, were he to accept the position, he might wish to do such an exhibition again. He replied that such an exhibition might be "a possibility" for whoever might be Curator. Six months later, Richard and I met again, this time to agree that he would become Curator of The Costume Institute, and again I posed "Costume: Period Rooms Re-Occupied in Style" as a concept. In Richard's reply, "a possibility" had become diminished to a profoundly dispassionate "I am sure it was beautiful," and I knew that I was not about to see my dream of mannequins posed in period rooms.

Nonetheless, I am delighted with "The Ceaseless Century: 300 Years of Eighteenth-Century Costume," a concept that allows us to see the luxury and persistence of eighteenth-century dress. One knows, of course, of

fig. 2

the rococo revival in the decorative arts and architecture, but this exhibition posits—for the first time, to my knowledge—a like recurrence of the eighteenth century in fashion. Subject to similar impulses in other visual arts, fashion was effected by the Goncourt espousal in the 1860s and 1870s of dix-huitième style; in the 1880s and 1890s, perhaps with fin-de-siècle yearnings, the bustle was often inflated into a semblance of the polonaise; in the 1910s, a softening silhouette remembered the transitional grace of the 1790s and the feathery laces of the eighteenth century; and Dior's New Look of 1947 catapulted the silhouette back into the eighteenth century, avoiding a recent history vitiated by holocaust and war. Today, designers such as Karl Lagerfeld for Chanel, Jean Paul Gaultier, and Stella McCartney for Chloe evoke the eighteenth century as a sumptuous fantasy and escape from modernism's temperance and discipline.

If the eighteenth century has escaped its period (and, I admit reluctantly, the period room) to endure into our time, we have a completely original approach to the style and perhaps one especially germane to the end of a century and millennium. Standing as we always do on the shoulders of giants, we see further and we recognize our indebtedness to the past. For three hundred years, the eighteenth century has stood for and crystallized our yearning for an effulgent beauty, flamboyance and artifice in silhouette, and the global resources of textiles and decoration. Perhaps these beautiful dresses need not inhabit our period rooms when we say with equal certitude that eighteenth-century costume yet dwells in our lives and desire—and yet again...

Philippe de Montebello
Director, The Metropolitan Museum of Art

It was the best of times, it was the worst of times, it was the age of wisdom, it was the age of foolishness, it was the epoch of belief, it was the epoch of incredulity, it was the season of Light, it was the season of Darkness, it was the spring of hope, it was the winter of despair, we had everything before us, we had nothing before us, we were all going direct to Heaven, we were all going direct the other way — in short, the period was so far like the present period, that some of its noisiest authorities insisted on its being received, for good or for evil, in the superlative degree of comparison only.

Charles Dickens (1812-70),
regarding the year 1775,
in *A Tale of Two Cities,* 1859

INTRODUCTION

The eighteenth century spirit abides. It lives in everyday contradiction and correlation of the kind that Dickens indicated in the nineteenth century. It has remained an option to be invoked whenever bourgeois modernity proves too grave or when the fireworks and majesty of an old order seem an antidote to the banality innate in modern life. In fashion, in particular, the eighteenth century is a model for dress of artifice and exuberance, ostentation and ornamentation, even as those elements atrophy in much modern clothing. The century might end at calendar's duration, but its dreamlike aura of opulence and of strong individualism within a structured society is ceaseless.

Of course, history is revived and revisited again and again in all the arts, in variations that range from the cold-hearted "roll over, Beethoven" type to a scrupulous historicism in which the authentic is barely distinguishable from the historicist copy. To return to the eighteenth century can be to retrieve the democratic ideals intrinsic in the values of the French and American Revolutions; to reconsider the aesthetics of the era can be to instill values of past practice and parameters. Architectural history is replete with historicism, and the rococo is as frequently used as any historical style, especially for the domestic appointments of the richest. Elsie de Wolfe's predilection for the epoch can easily be said to turn on her dislikes: "I loathe poverty. I hate the sordid, the ugly, and the cheap," for which the eighteenth century readily served as antonym. Such sovereign enclaves of the wealthy in America as Newport, Rhode Island, are unthinkable without the eighteenth century. Even museums in revival forms—most notably, the Museum's neighbor to the south, The Frick Collection—exercise authority from the regimen of an ancien régime setting, while our national heritage, exemplified by such sites as Colonial Williamsburg, is inscribed in eighteenth-century red brick.

Of course, any century of profound transition can be refracted into many mirrors of modern likeness, as Dickens did. Consider, in two small instances of costume historiography, the recent ways in which The Metropolitan Museum of Art has expressed costume. In 1963, in conjunction with the exhibition "Costume: Period Rooms Re-Occupied in Style," the Museum's accompanying text was accepting and exculpatory:

> During the 18th Century France had an almost complete monopoly of fashions. Growing out of the fairyland atmosphere of the French Court and conceived as often by ennui as by personal vanity, these fashions were a product of an age which sought at any price to live life with supreme grace. Reflecting the pursuit of this goal, the costumes were soft-colored, silken, elaborately trimmed and molded to fit into a world of gaiety and playfulness set into studied motion.... Women's costumes were shaped by a rigid corset and panniers worn to produce an extended hip effect which was thought to add dignity and grace in movement to court gowns. Made of either whalebone, cane or pliable wood, panniers were so indispensable that they were worn even in the most negligée toilette.... The costumes from the days of Louis XV and Louis XVI may seem frivolous and extravagant by our modern standards, but they have preserved for us textiles and embroideries of the highest order. They are heirlooms from an age which took the time to plan, to execute, and to enjoy things of great beauty and fine workmanship.

Nineteen years later, The Costume Institute exposed its eighteenth-century treasures again, this time accompanied by many significant loans from around the world, under the rubric "The Eighteenth-Century Woman." Even with the nuance of that title, the Museum's interpretation was inflected and perhaps more critical and dynamic than before. Special Consultant Diana Vreeland wrote in her introduction to the exhibition booklet:

> The century burst like a rose and spent itself lavishly, blowing its vitality in a strong and beautiful way all over the Western world. It was a century of quality, artistry, precision, and scholarship. Light, opportunity, and exultation were everywhere. The architecture, the porcelains, the gardens were sublime; every teacup and every flower was very special.... Our own concepts of architecture and decoration were established in the eighteenth

century. The interiors, the arrangements of the furniture, and the furniture itself were really all the first bloom of the way we live today. The comfort with which we live, the way a house is organized, the living in it, and the care of it were all creations of those days.... In the sixteenth and seventeenth centuries women definitely had power—if those around them were powerful and rich. But in the eighteenth century, women often found their way alone and with greater ease, as their talent was recognized and needed. They wrote books; they administered huge estates; they ran small businesses; they created salons where intellect and revolution found a place for expression; they ran convents, which were small worlds where women could live in great protection; and, of course, some women ruled great nations.

Vreeland's more subjective description betokens the near-score of years between the two exhibitions. By 1982, even the ideas of a great aesthete such as Vreeland had to lend recognition to gender generally and women specifically and to give pertinence to modern life. But Vreeland's ideas about a past germane to the present, even as specifically applied to the eighteenth century, do not stand alone. In her essay "Retro: A Reprise" from *The New Yorker* (1980), reprinted in *The Fashionable Mind* (1981), Kennedy Fraser perceived fashion historicism more cynically and caustically. Assessing her own time as troubled, she saw revival in fashion as a false panacea. "The fashions of the past continue to recur ... for the security blanket they provide in these times of terrible confusion. The past offers a vision of measurable, wrapped-up order. Fashion had its place, once upon a time, and its own clear rules.... Many fashion designers today ... are drawn time and again to the past as to a world of paradisal certainties." In Fraser's argument, fashion must be inevitably bold and forward-looking. Any glance backward renders one as Lot's wife. But that assumption is surely as false as it is frequently expressed.

Likewise, Gilles Lipovetsky has pointed out in *The Empire of Fashion* (1994) that fashion incarnates novelty and owes its central place in late twentieth-century life to the destiny of being unceasingly new. In a telling phrase, fashion is, for Lipovetsky, "the permanent theater of ephemeral metamorphoses." But fashion, as evidenced in the very forms and forces evident in the present exhibition, cannot entirely forget and defies being seen as novelty alone. If fashion defined the new, it would have to forsake its own past and the phenomena of retro and historicism that had molded fashion in the late twentieth century. It would be, at best, unjust to conclude, as Fraser has and as Lipovetsky might, from a false assumption of fashion's rapacious progressivism that fashion does not have the right that every other cultural expression has to negotiate with history.

To compare two explanatory exhibition texts, less than a score of years apart and representing the same institution, is to understand that fashion responds to both the objects and eras of the past, but also to some mercurial needs of its own time. A lesser image of fashion revivals prevails for the most part, but the possibility that fashion revisits with purpose and rectitude is important. While clothing's "cycles" and expressions in "retro" seem glibly and unimportantly reflective of the past, there is also a measure of fashion renaissance that is unerringly pointed and deliberately directed. Even Fraser hedged her bets and began to distinguish between nostalgia and historicism, explaining at the end of her essay that "staring into the far-distant past of design is a phenomenon of long enough standing in the history of fashion, after all. It seems more ominous to see some young designers choosing to revive sixties fantasies, miniskirts, and short white boots." In this, more circumspect, conclusion, Fraser may engage our consent, especially as we have been witness in the 1990s to wanton resurgences not only of the 1960s but even more dissolutely of the 1970s and 1980s.

In 1989, the exhibition and book *The Historical Mode* by Richard Martin and Harold Koda addressed fashion historicism in the 1980s. The nature of this exercise, which included a significant number of eighteenth-century examples, was very different from that of *The Ceaseless Century*. The earlier enterprise was to represent the swelled interest in historical references in 1980s art and fashion as an indication of modernism's détente and the history-embracing postmodernism ascendant in art and architecture. We did not, in that instance, seek out the continuity of interest but merely sought the parallels between the 1980s and specific historical periods.

Using the eighteenth century as its touchstone, *The Ceaseless Century* proceeds differently, not seeking the short distance between a discrete present and the multiple past but showing the complicated navigation that comes of revivalism swinging to and fro on the timeline of history and sensibility. Surely, we can understand the renewal of interest in eighteenth-century fashion in the 1980s in some larger twentieth-century context when we remember that the teens renewed the open gown, albeit on a more cylindrical silhouette, the twenties allowed for the robe de style with the lateral expansion of panniers, and the Dior New Look of 1947 reconstituted the desiderata of femininity in silhouette and of unabashed opulence in surface decoration. Then, as Vivienne Westwood, Jean Paul Gaultier, and Karl Lagerfeld for Chanel select exemplars out of the eighteenth century for their transfigured versions in the 1980s and 1990s, these designers still manifest a virtuoso knowledge of fashion history, but we know and they know that history did not stop in 1800 and await the reawakening of a 1980s sensibility. Thus, Barbara Baines's argument in *Fashion Revivals from the Elizabethan Age to the Present Day* (1981) that "revived and romantic styles of dress have always played an important role for the elite" is sustained. Her premise resides in the relationship between revivals and romanticism, broadly conceived. Baines proposed:

One indirect cause of this romantic dress may have been widespread dissatisfaction with what appeared to many Elizabethans to be a breakdown of traditional distinctions in dress. By assuming an esoteric and nostalgic guise which could only be achieved through education and courtly experience, the courtiers at the tilts were putting themselves beyond the reach of mere sumptuousness or parvenu expenditure; romance needs leisure to sustain it, as well as a sense of the past, and in dress is a means of eluding those who wish to imitate the appearance of mere wealth.

Baines is correct in knowing that historicism in dress is a distinction. For those who have naively thought The New Look new or who might mistake Westwood menswear that follows eighteenth-century patterns for a slipshod pajama, there are always those with the smug superiority to recognize historical sources. The sixteenth century revived grandiose armor and the panache of costume out of the Middle Ages and the Renaissance, abetted with a flair for the theatrical. Today we might choose to bring back an eighteenth-century silhouette and fabric with some sense that popular culture will not emulate such evocative extravagance.

Yet, Baines's model of elitism and exclusion through historical reference may be challenged by fashion-aware times. After all, the textiles of the 1880s and 1890s that harkened back to the eighteenth century extended those rare original textiles to a broader production and appreciation only made possible by the Industrial Revolution. Revivals in dress, as in any other form, favor conservatism and a cultural elite but, at a time of universal education, cannot be said to be only a romanticism for the prevailing power elite, even as a number of twentieth-century examples in this book answer more directly to an intellectual and avant-garde elite—albeit also an enlightened group—rather than to a privileged social class. Moreover, there are always distinctions to be made between a fossilized, buried-in-amber history and the past as premise to imagination and speculation.

In deliberate provocation, art historian Francis Haskell wrote in *Rediscoveries in Art* (1976): "The history of taste in the Old Masters begins in the 1840s." The self-consciousness of taste that Haskell described applies as well to architecture, interiors, garden design, and, of course, fashion, the often forgotten visual art. If there are collectors, connoisseurs, and decorators engaged in campaigns for historical awareness, one can only imagine that these recognitions of history would also apply to fashion, thus the resurgences in fashion that correspond to the Goncourt sensibility and others of the nineteenth century. Further, as Haskell pointed out, part of the power of those tastes of the nineteenth century was that they were often broadly communicated and disseminated, thus reaching not only the "happy few" but the masses as well. Fashion functioned in much the same way, its plates and ultimately its journals and magazines extending the outreach of dress while also following the privileged sensibility of the day. It is not surprising, therefore, to find the coalescences, even in English, French, and American examples, represented in this exhibition around the dix-huitième in the 1860s and again in the 1880s and 1890s. As cultural historian Daniel Roche has argued, the popular culture of clothing as consumption began immediately with the French Revolution. Where once there were rags, fashion was demanded.

Eighteenth-century fashion is unceasing because its principles in silhouette as artifice and in textile and surface as opulence are abidingly recalled in the history of fashion. Seldom the dominant sensibility, the dix-huitième offers itself as a miracle of rebirth at a time when extravagance, gilt, and sensuality may seem to be needed once again. Without the possibility of an eighteenth-century persistence, we would be immersed headlong in an ordinary world of minimalism, austerity, and unmitigated reason in dress (anachronistic dress and new, rational apparel were natural foes in the nineteenth century). With the eighteenth century as an option in taste, we do not presume to reconstitute aristocracy, but we may at least try to capture the emotions of a Mozart fantasia, the reason of philosophical treatise, the ordering of Diderot, and the elegant line of a Watteau rendering. Such an eighteenth century will always be elusive and complex, but also always well worth the aspiration and the sensation, and thus the "superlative degree of comparison only."

THE EIGHTEENTH CENTURY

The eighteenth century was itself a time not without memory. Its masques and remembrances of the seventeenth century were vivid, if occasionally comical. If we trust either Sir Joshua Reynolds or Johann Winckelmann, the canon of images to be retained was centuries old. If we observe the traffic that colonialism and world markets built, we know that cultures of dress were converging and each culture was gaining from the observation, whether admitting it or not. Thus, dress of the eighteenth century is not without anachronisms and exoticism of its own, but that singular, changing, revolutionizing century has become an icon in the history of fashion. As *The Ceaseless Century* posits, those hundred years or so that we have identified in unambiguous chronology and in ambiguous description have, at least in spirit, continued to live into our lives and times.

It is, of course, difficult to define not only the spirit of the century but also its dress. As fashion historian Aileen Ribeiro noted in her basic text, *Dress in Eighteenth Century Europe, 1715-1789,* most think immediately of Paris and the French court when they ponder that time, forgetting reverberations in England, Italy, and elsewhere worldwide. Admittedly, by the eighteenth century there was already an assumed supremacy in French taste, which has lingered into our own time. In real conflict, contradiction, and even political correctness regarding taste, we are likely to feel a keen affinity for that unceasing century.

The Ceaseless Century exhibition and book attempt to show and analyze great examples of eighteenth-century dress in the collection of The Costume Institute, The Metropolitan Museum of Art. In some sense, this could be a complete and fascinating enterprise in its own right. But herein the occasion is also taken to examine patterns of period revival that have occurred over the past two hundred years. There is both a dovetailing and a distinct difference in these two joint endeavors: we will see the eighteenth century best through its actual garments, but we may also see its shadow over time; revivals focus on and articulate the past, but they do so necessarily in terms of the needs of a later present. *The Ceaseless Century* is itself a revision and a revisiting; it takes the place of an exhibition planned for December 1997 that had the working title "The History of Fashion." That show, which was intended to consider revivals throughout the history of fashion, was postponed in order that we might respond to the death of Gianni Versace by presenting an analytical exhibition of the designer's work. As it happens, the

English. *Court dress (Robe à l'Anglaise, petticoat, stomacher),* detail of stomacher and front and back views, ca. 1760

Blue silk taffeta brocaded in wrapped and flat silver thread. Purchase, Irene Lewisohn Bequest, 1965 (CI 65.13.1 a-c)

This English gown of mid-century indicates the artifice of proportions sought in eighteenth-century dress. A rectangle of décolletage surmounts the triangular form of the stomacher, one of the separate elements of the dress. Highly detailed and decorated, the stomacher calls attention to its own form from the expansion at the bust for which it serves as perimeter for a tapering to and just below the waist. The visual effect is to make the waist seem delicate. Likewise, panniers trussed to and causing the broad dilation of the hips make the waist seem narrow within a mountain range of panniers. This garment is fifty-five inches wide; its prudent wearer eyed any doorway cautiously and negotiated most by entering sideways. At nearly six feet in breadth, this dress is basically flat, establishing the field of silver ornament, combining silk threads wrapped in silver and flat silver panels. The mid-eighteenth-century lady was as flattened out as road-kill, all the better to show off the decoration of clothing recognized as a two-dimensional field.

keystone of that exhibition was Versace's use of history, which included a considerable interest demonstrated in the eighteenth century. It was on preparing the Versace exhibition that I made the decision to recast "The History of Fashion" as a study of the eighteenth century and its influences and revivals, becoming far more restricted, but perhaps also far more explicit, than the original formulation for "the History of Fashion."

For the purposes of this venture, I chose at the outset certain signposts of eighteenth-century style that were intended not as single or certain semiotics but as cues that might be heeded. The majority of those cues arose in shapes and silhouettes. Dilated hips, especially as achieved by panniers, would be a point of attention. Likewise, the corseted waist, especially with extreme restriction of mobility as might be indicated by a center-front dip well below the natural waistline, should afford early warning. Correspondingly, the deep décolletage allowed by such infra-edifice would offer a sign of inner structure and of potential eighteenth-century reference. The drapery-parted opening of the skirt (open robe) to reveal underskirt, petticoat, or a like dress would always be a measure of eighteenth-century theatricality and sensuality. But one could not forget that the period of the 1780s and 1790s would provide a fin-de-siècle neoclassicism that must also be included as an indicator of the eighteenth century, if only in its final years. Polonaises and gatherings to flanks would be a sign as sure and as unsure as any other, but positively placed on the screen of attention.

In textiles and surface ornament, there were also preliminary expectations of style that were more or less borne out. I knew that silks

might transmogrify, but that rococo patterns would abide and that late-century stripes with pattern might retain their allure. I expected linens, those creamy and tactile luxuries of eighteenth-century textile better known outside the court, might haunt later dressmakers' imaginations. Embroidery, never defunct and itself an art of preserved patterns of ways of working and seeing, could be telling of a proclivity to eighteenth-century origins if and when, in style and placement, it accorded with the paradigms of sumptuous costume in the ancien régime. Through the example of embroidery, I knew too that we would remember menswear as well as womenswear and would have to allow for crossover, as one always does in the history of dress. Further, the ancient art of lace and of linens and fichus applied to dress would have to be remembered.

But the last thing one would want would be a pattern book for eighteenth-century derivations that, when matched with a subsequent garment, required one to shout "Eureka." On the contrary, the matches and the affinities in dress must be, in the best Dickensian way, solid enough for a legal proof and subtle enough for no proof to be needed because one is already a true believer. Perhaps the rationality of the eighteenth century might have warranted a more scientific method, but the caprice and commitment of historicism proffered the more emotional and instinctive process.

Moreover, I knew where to look on a timeline but did not want to ignore any possibilities that did not meet my preconception. After all, the decorative arts and architectural history led me inexorably to the 1860s, the 1890s, the 1910s and 1920s, and postmodernism in the 1980s and

French. *Robe à la Francaise (open robe and petticoat),* back view, late 1770s-1780s
Green and white striped silk/linen blend.
Purchase, Irene Lewisohn Bequest, 1965
(CI 65.13.2 a-c)

French. *Robe à l'Anglaise (open robe and petticoat),* back view, 1785-87
Pink and white striped silk taffeta.
Purchase, Irene Lewisohn Bequest, 1966
(CI 66.39 a,b)

Whereas the court dress of two decades earlier had contrived to make broad planar fields, the style of the 1770s lifted and agitated the robe to facilitate movement. Even the court was smitten by the philosophy of Jean-Jacques Rousseau and the advancement of nature; clothing was now for walking almost as much as for ceremony. The means to achieve mobility was hitching up the skirt, in the style often known as "retrousée dans les poches," or tucked up through the pockets. The look was thereby no longer of a rigid plane craving ornamentation but of an agitated, almost baroque sculpture of fluid forms gathering near the waist.

Stripes matching in open robe and petticoat give unity and a relatively simple formality to this 1780s dress. Lacking the embellishments of many earlier and contemporary dresses, this one employs self-fabric pinked ruffles on the petticoat. A narrow waist is emphasized, as the robe ends in flaps below the natural waist. The bust is also most prominent, probably veiled only by the lace or sheer mull fichu along the arcing display of deep décolletage.

English. *Robe à la Francaise,*
detail and side view, ca. 1760

*Blue silk damask brocaded with polychrome
silks in a floral pattern. Bequest of
Catherine D. Wentworth, 1948 (TSR
48.187.709 a,b)*

This open robe with matching petticoat
of about 1760 is one of the paradigms
for eighteenth-century revivals. It
possesses salient features: robe-like
enclosure over a petticoat, heavy
ornamentation of the border of the robe
top to bottom, broadened hips and
contrasting narrow waist, and luxurious
materials made even more so by their
juxtapositions.

1990s. Painting, particularly because of the academy's waning force,
seemed a less reliable set of dates to check. In fact, the decorative arts and
architecture divining rod yielded much and was viable, but it failed to
provide the full catch that this study entailed. So, criteria existed, but were
flexible; expectations existed but were not to be relied upon exclusively.
But at a certain point, anyone figures out where the fish are biting.

There are many aspects of The *Ceaseless Century* that cannot be
included in an eighty-page book. Millinery is absent here as it also is
largely in the exhibition, where all the mannequins' heads are being
swathed in like material to enhance the resemblance among periods. But
hats tell that story with certainty. Thus, in the exhibition, three giant
cartwheel hats will suffice to show an abiding interest in the same shape.
A flat felted-wool cartwheel from about 1750, a grand flat-crowned disk
of the early nineteenth century in leghorn straw, and a Balenciaga tan
straw cartwheel of about 1953, perfect for averting one's eyes in a
Richard Avedon photograph, constitute an unerring straight line in the
history of fashion. Almost interchangeable, these accessories are principal
and enthralling.

The elegant life of the eighteenth century was lived among
mirrors that reflected the immediate, and some would say ephemeral,
radiance of fashion. Those mirrors also constitute a metaphorical glass of
history, glimpses, icons, and suggestions that persist through reflection
and imagination into our own time.

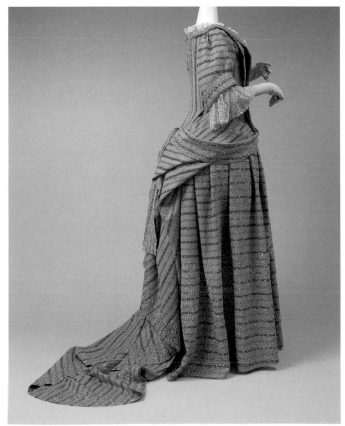

English. *Mantua and petticoat,*
detail, front view, back view,
side view, and front cover right,
1690-95
Light-brown striped wool embroidered
with metal thread. Rogers Fund, 1933
(TSR 33.54 a,b)

A late seventeenth-century version of the
open robe and the earliest piece in this
exhibition, this two-piece dress is richly
decorated with embroidery in silver gilt
thread. If it looks little like our
preconception of eighteenth-century
court dress, the anomaly is in part a
sedateness, perhaps more grave than
many of the wearer's later rococo sisters.
Moreover, this sensible wool costume is
for winter and lacks the deep décolletage
and bright silks of spring and summer
attire. In 1695, a lady of the French court
complained that women were turning
blue from the cold when required to wear
silk dresses in winter.

American. *Robe à la Polonaise (open robe and petticoat),* back view and detail, 1780-85

Hand-painted yellow Chinese silk. Gift of Heirs of Emily Kearney Rodgers Cowenhoven, 1970 (1970.87 a,b)

Hand-painted Chinese silks were among the most coveted and refined materials for dresses of the eighteenth century; European copies were made in the dearth of the prized Chinese originals. This example, said to have belonged to the family of Jonathan Belcher, colonial governor of New Jersey from 1747 to 1757, could not have entered the Colonies directly from China because of trade restrictions, but may have come through England. Conforming now to the new style of the polonaise, draping the skirt in a copious and slack back drape and side swaggers or pouches, the volumetric form affords an apparent opposition to the beauty of the textile and its hand-painting. One could almost wish for the return of the 1750s and 1760s mode of road-kill planarity to display the flower painting. As it is, much is lost in the deep troughings and agitation of the drapery.

French. *Robe à la Francaise,* detail
and front view, ca. 1770
Striped ivory silk faille brocaded with
polychrome floral pattern. Purchase, Irene
Lewisohn Bequest, 1961 (CI 61.13.1a,b)

A low neckline, wide and relatively flat
panniers, and an abundance in kinds and
quantity of decoration characterize the
ball gown of this time. Self-fabric
embellishments and fly fringe are in
profusion, adding to the intense color,
activity, and liveliness of the lavish and
busy textile. Not only for cultural reasons
of the French court but also because they
are so declarative of individual certainty
and social authority, dresses such as this
have become the icon and cinematic
standard for eighteenth-century style.
They are an anticipation of what is later
called in fashion "the full Cleveland," or
style apogee.

English. *Robe à la Francaise (open robe and petticoat),* **front view and two details, 1740s**

Hand-painted cream silk moiré faille, crocheted netting, cream silk fly fringe, and polychrome flowers of silk floss. Purchase, Harris B. Dick fund, 1995 (1995.235 a,b)

This quintessential and extraordinarily beautiful *robe à la Francaise* with a full repertory of panniered skirt and corseted waist embodies the style: two box pleats on the back (see detail) stitched down from neckline to shoulder blades form a Watteau or sacque back; self-fabric robings at center front promote the extravagance of the hand-painting; fly fringe and silk-floss flowers add another layer and a garden effect to the horror vacui of ornamentation throughout. Like the 1770s example preceding (pp. 26-27), this dress suggests the taste for an excess of richnesses. After all, it is Dr. Samuel Johnson, eighteenth-century British lexicographer, critic, and conversationalist, to whom the echoing line "It is better to live rich than to die rich" is attributed. This dress foregoes no possibility of lush elaboration, no pleasure either two-dimensional or three-dimensional.

French. *Pierrot bodice,* detail and
side view, ca. 1785
*Warp-patterned striped silk/linen blend of
cream, yellow, pink, and green. Courtesy
Martin Kamer*

Differentiated from the full-fledged
Pierrot costume, the Pierrot as a shaped
bodice flourishes in that last gasp of
rococo sensibility and extreme silhouette
of about 1780-1790. The flared peplum
extension of the jacket below the waist
asymmetrically around the back allows
for the bulbous, billowing skirt of the
period. Self-fabric ruffles on the bodice
make it almost a condensed version of the
open robe of this period and slightly
earlier: the self-fabric ruffles would have
characterized the skirt, but the Pierrot
bodice includes even those ruffles. The
simple low-necked bodice is characteristic
of the period, comparable to the *chemise à
la reine.*

English. *Dress,* back view, side
view, and detail, ca. 1735

*Brown silk satin with polychrome weft
patterning. Purchase, Irene Lewisohn Bequest,
1964 (CI 64.14)*

A Spitalfields silk dress with a dome-
shaped skirt conforms not only to the
silhouette of the 1730s but also to the
interaction between silks and laces during
that time, especially evident in Spitalfields
manufacture. The silk pattern is like that
of lace. While such interaction seems
hard to imagine between worker and
pattern book, clothing is a place where
the various media ultimately converge.
Eighteenth-century dress, in particular,
was a *Gesamtkunstwerk* of artisanal and
dressmaking skills. While most
eighteenth-century dresses have been
altered in some way for subsequent use,
fashion historian Janet Arnold has noted
that this dress shows no sign of ever
having been altered and is thus in its
perfect original state.

Italian. *Afternoon dress,* detail and
back view, ca. 1795
Dark-green and violet striped silk with white
brocaded border. Purchase, Irene Lewisohn
Bequest, 1979 (1979.20 a,b)

By the 1790s, the structure of clothing
was undergoing dramatic change. This
afternoon dress in the form of a round
gown steadfastly keeps up appearances
and can pass for eighteenth-century
opulence, especially in its colors and
textile richness, but high-waisted dress,
spencer, corset, and separate sleeves are
effectively a new anatomy, one that
anticipates the century to come.
Similarly, this shape would be renewed in
many ways in the 1880s and 1890s,
when one fin-de-siècle recapitulated the
preceding fin-de-siècle.

English. *Robe à la Polonaise (robe and petticoat),* back view and detail, ca. 1780.

Cream linen with polychrome chintz appliqué, gold embroidery and metal sequins.
Courtesy Martin Kamer

The element of eighteenth-century fashion that we think of first is probably the court style. This linen dress of great beauty, and also of simplicity, provincialism, and even a degree of vulgarity compared to court dress, is most instructive. The bodice and skirt sewn together constitute a robe; a matching petticoat is worn underneath. Heavy linen, almost of a diaper weight and of great tactility, will always feel luxurious, but it also bears a common touch. Likewise, the floral appliqué is clumsy and garish, rather oversized for the dress, especially when compared with such refined examples as the embroidered cottons of the 1780s and 1790s of court style (see pp. 38-39). But this country cousin possesses her own charm, and the dressmaking is sure. If a few roses loom too large and the reinforcement with metal sequins strikes one as grossly vernacular, one must remember that even high style in the emerging age of fashion plates and periodicals is not uniform and does not always conform to our ideal of good taste.

European. *Dress (open robe, petticoat, and fichu),* detail and side view, ca. 1798
Fine Indian mull embroidered with polychrome silk thread. Purchase, Irene Lewisohn and Alice L. Crowley Bequests, 1992 (1992.119.1 a-c)

English. *Round gown,* side view, ca. 1798
White cotton with polychrome wool crewel embroidery. Funds from various donors, 1998 (1998.222.1)

It is the combination of elements within this costume that makes it so interesting. Embroidered, open-fronted robes with matching underskirts are more usually associated with the 1760s to 1780s, but the train and the tiny bodice, only two and one-half inches from neckline to waist, preclude any date earlier than about 1798. The matching fichu is extremely rare. Each piece is embroidered with variations on the floral designs rather than mere duplications, suggesting artisanal primacy, not pattern book repetitions. This dress is believed to have belonged to Catherine Beekman (1762-1839), wife of Elisha Boudinot of Princeton, New Jersey.

The round gown of the 1790s stands just before the complete renunciation of three-dimensional shaping and color in the First Empire, more or less imitating Greek sculpture bereft of polychromy (as it was often seen and envisioned in the eighteenth century). Delicate polychrome wool crewel embroidery saves this dress from the austerity of the later style and assures a date of about 1798; the piece fully anticipates the Empire style but retains one last vestige of rococo ornament and incident.

French. *Robe à l'Anglaise (open robe and petticoat),* **two back views and detail, ca. 1784-87**
White muslin embroidered with silver metallic tinsel. Isabel Shults Fund, 1991 (1991.204 a,b)

Structure and silhouette were all-important in the eighteenth century. Cotton emerged as a fashionable fabric in the 1780s with the *chemise à la reine,* the cotton shift favored by Marie Antoinette beginning in this turbulent decade. As always, clothing had profound political and international implications. Marie Antoinette may have been posing in *déshabille* and a single layer as someone sincere and real instead of one who follows the customs of the imitative and regal. But she was also infuriating the Lyons silk manufacturers, jettisoning their extravagant outer layer and choosing to aggrandize cottons imported from India. On such grounds this new clothing was highly controversial. But the cotton dress was no plain Jane: its shape was still the *robe à l'Anglaise,* and the muslin was gathered to ample and enduring shape. Fifteen to twenty years later, cotton and muslin dresses would be slack and sheer by choice, just as this one still conforms to the prevailing shape.

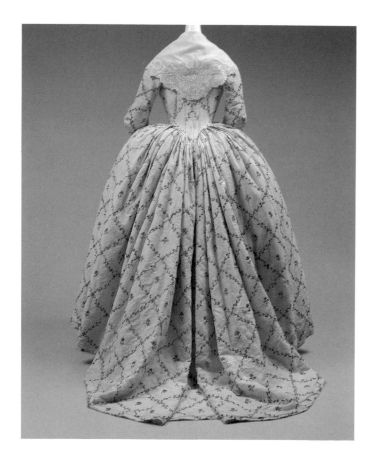

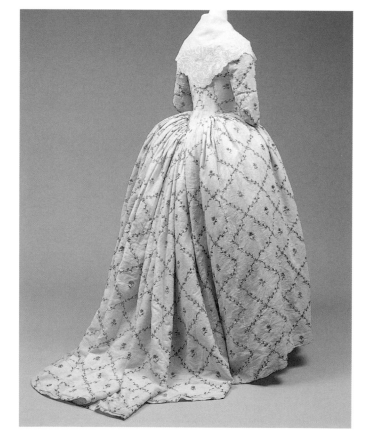

French. *Robe à la Francaise (open robe and petticoat),* detail and back view, 1760-70

Polychrome warp-printed Chiné silk taffeta. Purchase, Irene Lewisohn Bequest, 1960 (CI 60.40.2 a,b)

Standard European silhouettes of the eighteenth century accommodated a world of change and specifically a changing world dominated by new textile techniques from Asia and the Middle East. This French textile emulates *ikat* (a technique in which yarns are tie-dyed before weaving) in a manner then known as a result of a geographic mistake as *chiné.* The softened edges of the *ikat* do not mitigate a bold textile design, nor do they entirely surrender to the authority of the Western shaping. Pinked-edge pleated and ruched self-fabric (see detail) trace the form of the open robe. An eighteenth-century template of dress is all but unchanging, yet the influence of new material requires a syncretism. In terms of eighteenth-century revivals, it is important to recognize how much the classic forms of eighteenth-century dress accommodated translations into arresting new textile forms in the 1760s and even the new textiles in the cottons of the 1780s.

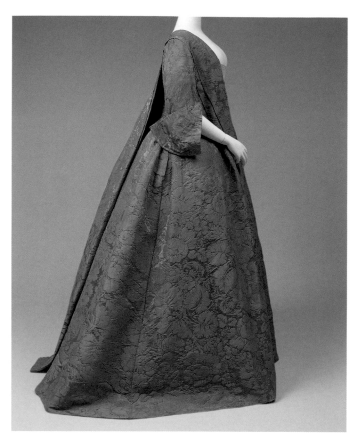

French. *Robe à la Française,* side view, ca. 1735-40

Brown silk damask. Gift of Mary Tavener Holmes, 1983 (1983.399.1)

This open robe, lacking petticoat, in spice brown damask reveals both the wide circumstance of the 1730s style, just before the flattening out at mid-century, and the hedonism of extraordinary damask, even when monochromatic. The luxury in this textile art alone is enough to warrant the interest in and satisfaction from this open robe.

American. *Dress,* side view and detail, 1790s

Pink taffeta with fine stripes of cream silk and metallic thread brocaded with metallic sprigs, pink taffeta. Courtesy Cora Ginsburg

By the 1790s, the high-waisted cylinder that would become the standard of the Empire had begun to prevail, depriving fashion of its century-long exercise in inflated, extended, and rigid shapes. If the great origami of artifice in three dimensions was relaxed, the play of textiles in the 1790s remained lavish and lush. Pink taffeta with metallic sprigs is a far cry from the tabula rasa of the all-white world of early Empire style, exemplified by Jacques-Louis David's portrait of *Madame Récamier* (1800). This dress has a provenance from the Plumstead/Rush/Campbell families of Philadelphia.

American. *Robe à l'Anglaise (round gown),* **back view, ca. 1775**
Emerald-green silk damask. Purchase, Irene Lewisohn Trust Fund, 1994 (1994.406 a-c)

Spitalfields silk, rich in textile reference and opulent as a material, was used to create this elegant round gown. Initially shown by The Metropolitan Museum of Art in an exhibition of John Singleton Copley's American portraits, it conveys the spirit of those polished, lustrous, proud figures and interiors one associates with Copley's portraiture. For the Colonials, an unspoken elegance was more important than ostentatious display, yet anyone possessing such rich material would inevitably be glorious or proud.

Italian. *Dress panels à la disposition,* **detail of one of four, 1780-90**
Green-yellow silk satin embroidered with polychrome silk floss and metal sequins. Purchase, Isaac Fletcher Fund by exchange and Irene Lewisohn Charitable Trust, 1998 (1998.191 a-d)

Four panels of green-yellow silk satin, cut and embroidered *à la disposition,* were prepared to create a gown and petticoat but were never made up. In the unusual instance of having all the pieces, we have simulated in the exhibition the actual garment that would have been made. Of course, in doing this, we know we recapitulate Diderot in showing both process (and that preeminently) and result. The Costume Institute has a number of other uncut *à la disposition* silks. In presenting this grouping in *The Ceaseless Century,* we hope to represent the analytical process that accompanied the exceptional artisanal skill of the era.

THE NINETEENTH CENTURY

The nineteenth century was marked by waves of revival and eclecticism. As Charles Dickens knew well, the future beckoned, and technology, industry, and business drove a fast-moving society. Yet always with the ebb of yearnings for the past came memories of bygone times and even periodic Luddite rejections of the new in favor of a perceived "old." The political principles by which the old hegemonies were reviled would occasionally give way to a nostalgia, as some old aristocrats sought restoration and a new bourgeoisie was intrigued by privileges and luxuries no longer attainable. In this complex process, the eighteenth century was never forgotten and never far from the ambitions of both those who advocated the conservative course and those who preferred the progressive path.

There was, however, a significant hiatus between the eighteenth century and its revivals. In fact, there was no substantive presence of eighteenth-century dress revival until the 1860s, at which time sufficient distance had been established to gainsay the present with some not-personally-remembered but burnished and legendary sense of the past. The eighteenth century might well have been invoked for its politics during the Bourbon Restoration, for its regimen in dress and civility in the crisis of manners that occurred in the 1820s and 1830s, as is evidenced in the United States by the vulgarity of Andrew Jackson's rampantly proletarian and democratic presidency. But even those most dismayed by Jacksonian populism or its counterpart in rough and rural sensibilities elsewhere seem never to have invoked the politically incorrect and too-close eighteenth century as a time of civilized behaviors and rules of apparel. So we learn that time not only heals; it is also a vintage elixir, best administered after at least two generations.

The Second Empire brought the first profound and protracted renewal of eighteenth-century fashion. Imperial ambitions might be implicitly fostered by an old style rendered new. Equally characteristic of the Second Empire was the manner in which this revival style, redolent of the ancien régime, could seem thoroughly modern and democratic as well. In a way similar to Baron Georges Eugène Haussmann's inventive, but evocative, majestic improvements of Paris, the women on the balconies and at the carrefours might be dressed in the manner of the eighteenth century, but they appeared to be preeminently modern. The crystal palaces of crinoline, providing an airy shaping of silhouette without the oppressive massing of past fashion, were key to the view of 1860s apparel. As ambitious as the city's plan, dress of the Second Empire expressed itself as historical without being passé.

Revue de la Mode, October 1887

Elíse. English. *Ball gown,* front view and detail, ca. 1880

Blue machine-lace over cream silk, white organdy over gold lamé, gold braid trim, lace and silk flowers. Courtesy Martin Kamer

Emphatically in the style of an eighteenth-century open robe with petticoat, this nineteenth-century version is different in its bodice construction and trained skirt but startlingly alike in appearance. The waistband reads "by special appointment, Dressmaker to H.R.H. the Princess of Wales/Elise, 170 Regent Street, London." Elise has captured all the details of eighteenth-century style as well as the general effect: lace engageants extend the set-in sleeves; the neckline is edged with lace; and a bouquet of red silk flowers plays off the frequent incorporation of fresh flowers in eighteenth-century dress.

Concomitantly, fashion was emerging during these same decades from the practices of dressmakers and artisanal trades (as classified, of course, by Diderot in the eighteenth century) to become a modern phenomenon. What had been the privileges of court style in the eighteenth century were now becoming available, either in replication or in some less expensive rendering, to bourgeois women. (Men had largely forsaken all prior style for that related to the full blast of nineteenth-century industry and commerce.) With the coming of the sewing machine and new technologies, many of the effects of composite dressing, largely simplified during the first fifty years of the century, could be restored or made to look similar. Both the new industry of ready-to-wear and the newly organized haute couture showed off their profligate skills, garnishing and embellishing dress to a point that the nineteenth century came even to exceed the earlier century in its extravagances, bare-shouldered licentiousness, and rich colors (now enabled through chemistry). There was clearly a delirium of possibilities not only to achieve the supreme sumptuousness of eighteenth-century fashion but even to surpass it.

In the nineteenth century, the prior hundred years were remembered and honored in textiles that directly emulate earlier materials, though often substituting prints for wovens. In The Costume Institute, for example, numerous late-nineteenth-century textiles are virtual look-alikes for textiles of our eighteenth-century garments. The stunningly unapologetic revivalism of an 1880s English print (pp. 52-53), for example, speaks to the very willing association with past textiles.

English. *Dress,* detail and back view, ca. 1882-83

Printed cream cotton with shepherdess in medallion motif. Gift of The New-York Historical Society, 1979 (1979.346.43 a,b)

The nineteenth century found inspiration in the silhouettes of the prior century. But such interest might be pursued with a perverse imagination, as in this instance. A demure bodice worthy of the nineteenth century is attenuated here below the waist to curve back and divide, but with the sense of an open gown. The side panels sweep up to a flamboyant back panel that arches into what is a cross between a polonaise and a flying buttress. This cotton dress, very presumptuous and dramatic in silhouette, is complemented by its textile of naive rococo-evoking medallions with shepherdess and lambs.

In the nineteenth century the most conspicuous form of eighteenth-century costume was chosen as the paradigm for revival. The open robe reappeared again and again with glamor and theatricality. Indeed, in some Victorian dresses the open gown resembles stagecraft with open curtains as much as any example from fashion. Having chosen the most evident example in dress, nineteenth-century style only aggrandized the effect of the prior century. This was not a let-well-enough-alone attitude or a reverential act of preservation; it was a willful act of hyperbole and exaggeration.

Details like ruching, ribbons, and laces not only followed the eighteenth-century paradigm but went to great extremes. Ribbons and tyings associated with stomachers in authentic eighteenth-century dress could almost appear at will in nineteenth-century versions. Lace, now either machinemade or handmade, proliferated at all levels of fashion.

The buoyant sweep of the polonaise was the most notable silhouette device copied in the nineteenth century. This floating form of material that always reveals another layer or underdress beneath was taken into the vocabulary of lighter dress in the 1870s and after. Likewise, by the latter part of the nineteenth century, Gainsborough hats (which would ironically continue to appear in the early works of Picasso and Matisse) with broad brims, tilted elegance (if properly worn), and festive plumage comprised a self-conscious revival of the eighteenth century. Men's top hats atrophied and began to be models for women's millinery, simply taking on a new scale.

While a "proper" coat-like bodice with buttoning at center front has supplanted the accustomed deep décolletage of the previous century, every other aspect of this 1872 wedding dress emulates the eighteenth century. Self-trims, lace, ribbon, and even orange blossoms re-create the repertoire of dress techniques from a century earlier. As the technology and techniques emerged in the 1860s and 1870s that could make any dressmaker a virtuoso of eighteenth-century style, fashions such as these could be created. Would this have been a poor person's version of the eighteenth century? In a sense, the bourgeois access to the old forms of aristocracy in dress had to wait until the Second Empire and then, abetted by technology, arrived with a vengeance. Of course, the truism is that wedding dresses tend to be conservative and even retardataire; but the gap is not often the full century or more that it is here.

Thus, the century of eclecticism waited some fifty years before honoring its antecedent century, but once the eighteenth century form became an option for revival, it became more prevalent and powerful than that of any other period.

Of course, in the nineteenth century, the present and past were in such consonance and conjunction that it may sometimes be hard to see the sources lurking in the progression of nineteenth-century style. For some, the bustle of the 1880s can be that form and no other, not even the polonaise of the eighteenth century. Yet in examples in this chapter (and particularly in the summer dress on page 55), one sees distinctly that the dilation of cloth at the posterior is gathered with the same swathing and wrapping of the polonaise, not the bustle's full disposition of mass toward the back. Further, that this device is invariably accompanied by other telling traits of the dix-huitième substantiates the anachronism that seems to be so apt.

Few have noted and not all may even agree today that the eighteenth century had a profound influence in the second half of the nineteenth century, a fact attributable to the devious intertwining of history and the contemporary that occurred at that time.

In the 1850s, Théophile Gautier extolled Ingres's ceiling painting of the Apotheosis of Napoleon I for the Hotel de Ville, Paris. He declared it worthy of "the age of Pericles or of Augustus." In offering a standard of antiquity, he was praising a painting that is a kind of eighteenth-century revival for Ingres, the canny painter of many historicist styles. To be so oblique as to praise the style of the eighteenth

American. *Day ensemble*, back
view, ca. 1869
*Blue and white striped silk taffeta trimmed
with self fabric ruching. Gift of Deane and
Sydney Litwalk, 1984 (1984.594 a-d).*

American. *Summer walking dress,*
back view, ca. 1885
*Cotton with geometric and floral whitework
trim. Funds from various donors, 1998
(1998.222.2 a,b)*

By the late 1860s, this homage to the
eighteenth century could only have been
conceived and made with some
intentionality and disposition to the
historical. Eighteenth-century ruching
flutters and balloons out the back of the
overskirt to allow for the skirt's full
volume. The striped taffeta with self-
devices for decoration reinforces the
presence of the eighteenth century. By
the 1860s the sewing machine and other
apparel technology offered extravagance
in decoration for a newly modest cost.
This dress seeks to include every flourish
and luxury of the eighteenth century
hitherto unaffordable in nineteenth-
century bourgeois clothing. Ironically,
new technology was first used to
emulate old styles.

Eighteenth-century dress had already
enjoyed one revival in the 1860s and was
being renewed in the 1880s with further
publication of the Goncourt *Journals* and
also with the vogue for a modified
polonaise that was becoming confused
with the evolution of the bustle. The
sweeping ease of such a summer dress of
the 1880s is in some ways more readily
associated with the fluffy and pushed-up
1780s style than with the formality and
rigidity of the tea-set bustle that
originated in the 1880s.

American. *Young girl's ball gown ensemble,* back view, ca. 1872
Pink silk taffeta trimmed with cream tarlatan and silk fringe. Gift of Richard Martin, 1998 (1998.235.4 a-f)

Very probably part of a mother-daughter pair of ball gowns, this gown may suggest the aggressiveness of its era and/or an intimation of "fancy dress" or deliberate historical styling. It is not so self-conscious as to become Martha Washington to Dolley Madison, but the time from post-Civil-War to Centennial America was steeped in the spirit of eighteenth-century revival, above all for nationalistic reasons. Of course, it is hard to reconcile a bubble-gum pink with the mandates of national pride. Surely, revival was in the air (see p. 57) in the 1870s and may have constituted an aesthetic choice alone.

century by classical reference in the middle of the nineteenth century is the very complexity we approach. But we know that the nineteenth century consumed history with voracity. And the eighteenth-century taste is always delectable and irresistible.

Mon. Vignon. French. *Evening
dress,* side and front views,
ca. 1877

*Ecru and gold silk brocade with green velvet,
ecru satin, passementerie, and frosted bugle-
bead trim. Gift of Mary Pierrepont Beckwith,
1969 (CI 69.14.12a,b)*

Uncannily like the dresses in the
wonderfully presumptuous portraits of
John Singer Sargent and Thomas Eakins
of the same time, this 1870s evening
dress extracts the full glitz and glamor of
eighteenth-century fashion for a new
epoch. Ornament crowds out other
ornament; the configuration of the open
robe is renewed; its silhouette is bold and
begins to connect the eighteenth century
with its Belle Époque revival.

American. *Dress,* front view, side view, and detail, 1876-78

Dark-brown wool serge with tan and cream embroidery and brown taffeta trim. Gift of Mrs. Charles Edward Freet, 1939 (CI 39.68)

The most salient feature of eighteenth-century appropriation demonstrated in this dress is its long line of embroidery at center front and descending to the hem. The floral decoration and its placement on the garment arise not from copying eighteenth-century women's fashion but from a comprehension of eighteenth-century menswear. It is as if the waistcoat's ebullient decorative impulse has been transferred to the brown wool of this almost too-dour nineteenth-century dress.

THE TWENTIETH CENTURY

Fancy dress and masquerade had provided powerful release from the moment for eighteenth-century men and women of style. Two centuries later, fancy dress and masquerade would be strong elements in the persistence of eighteenth-century style. As Aileen Ribeiro has written in *The Dress Worn at Masquerades in England, 1730 to 1790, and Its Relation to Fancy Dress in Portraiture,* "Although in essence, the masquerade portrait is an ephemeral one, in the 18th century it was allied to the fashion for being painted in 'historical' dress that would outlast current modes and that would have a universal appeal; it was a revelation of people's aspirations and the way in which they saw themselves." So, too, the twentieth century has taken textile, silhouette, adornment, and even narrative from eighteenth-century fashion, often assuming its historical but timeless role, as exemplary.

The art of the eighteenth century has also provided inspiration. The spring-summer 1985 collection of Chanel by Karl Lagerfeld, for example, included a suit taken directly (but adapted) from Watteau's memorable *Pierrot,* or *Gilles* (ca. 1718-19) and also less direct versions of the artist's work, evening coats with Watteau backs. Vivienne Westwood appropriates images from Boucher (p. 74). But fashion itself is the primary stimulus to the revival forms. Panniers that are structurally similar to those of the eighteenth century are employed by Lanvin in her politely expansive robes de style. Embroideries of the era are matched by Lagerfeld for Chanel (pp. 64-65) and by Pierre Balmain (pp. 62-63).

For designers such as Lagerfeld and Versace (front cover left), the eighteenth century is very much associated with sexuality. Like contemporary filmmakers, many of whom are drawn to the period more for tight breeches, loose chemises, and deep décolletages, as well as lusty lives and licentious court intrigues, there is a passion about the eighteenth century that subsequent Victorianism and modernism all but suppressed. The open robe became a showgirl's strut rather than the coy metaphor of parted curtains. One must recognize, though, that this late-century view is different from the sweet allegiance of Boué Soeurs (p. 74) and Lanvin (p. 72) to a robe-de-style elegance and propriety.

A 1912 dress with polonaise, self-bordered fabric in stripes, lace inserts, and even the bouquet of flowers associated with the eighteenth-century corsage (pp. 66-67) shows a complete, almost textbook, loyalty to the past. Olivier Theyskens's trailing whirlwind of vintage linen and open robe exposed to a miniskirt (back cover) is a tour de force of

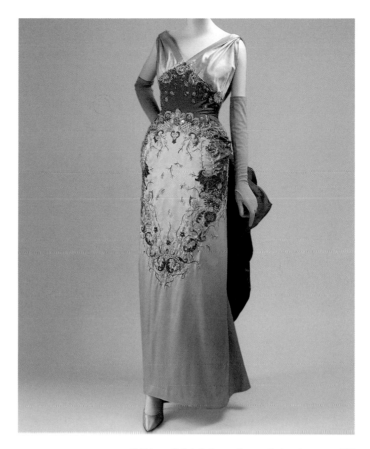

Pierre Balmain. *Evening dress,*
detail and front view, fall-winter
1954-55

Ivory silk satin and brown silk taffeta
with pearl, seed bead, sequin, and shell
embroidery. Gift of Mrs. David Rosenthal,
1960 (CI 60.30)

In the 1950s, the dix-huitième revival
launched by Dior flourished in the
French couture. In individual and
idiosyncratic ways, designers such as
Jacques Fath, Cristobal Balenciaga, and
the demure Pierre Balmain rendered their
versions of the eighteenth century. For
Balmain, consistently discreet, the
eighteenth century signified the quiet
luxury of the most sumptuous and varied
embroidery. The eye would be dazzled,
but with judgment and an unassuming
pleasure. An earlier twentieth-century
counterpart might be the Jean-Philippe
Worth gown (1900-1905) on pp. 68-69.

contemporary sensibility, faithful to the original yet willing to see it exposed
and deconstructed in order to become fresh and new again. These antithetical
impulses, some eighty-six years apart in time, speak to twentieth-century
circumstances as much as they honor the eighteenth century.

The century that modernity and modernism have propelled has
appealed throughout, but especially in the teens, 1920s, 1950s, 1980s,
and 1990s, to the eighteenth century for its refuge, pre-modern and
pre-bourgeois. So frequent is the recourse we have had to the
eighteenth century that the time long ago is very much a part of our
values today.

When artist David Hockney received his graduation award from
the Royal College of Art in London for a trip to the United States, he
knew that his would be a personal version of Hogarth's *Rake's Progress*
(and he so named a series of prints), a certainty even before he took the
trip. Models of living, the novel or narrative of life itself, were ordained
in the eighteenth century and remain operative today. We do not
simply step into eighteenth-century styles because of the masquerade,
but rather to avoid the transient and momentary that everywhere
prevail in our lives. When we are on occasion bold enough to grasp for
the eternal, we seize it through the eighteenth century. Dior's quest to
find a world not vitiated by holocaust and war led him back two
hundred years. Versace and Lagerfeld's circumventions of sexual
propriety and guilt lead them back two hundred years. And anyone
who might seek beauty and order in our unquiet century might well
think first and foremost of the eighteenth century.

Chanel by Karl Lagerfeld. *Evening ensemble,* front view and detail, fall-winter 1990-91
Cream silk satin decorated with embroidered appliqué of gold braid and metallic thread.
Gift of Mouna Al-Rashid, 1996
(1996.129a-i)

Lagerfeld, who has taken the eighteenth century as a Leitmotif of his art and life from residences and domestic interiors, to his fashion, and even to a brief personal whim of powdering his hair, has seized the bravura assertion from the court gown, opening up at center front. For Lagerfeld, the condensed and ironic image is both Versailles and showgirl, aristocracy and vulgarity. Other Lagerfeld for Chanel references to the eighteenth century include the 1980s Watteau-back gowns and the 1985 *Pierrot,* or *Gilles* suit derived from the Watteau painting.

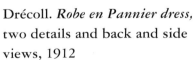

Drécoll. *Robe en Pannier dress,*
two details and back and side
views, 1912
Yellow silk taffeta with blue and cream
stripes, blue velvet, cream embroidered net, and
silk flowers. Courtesy Martin Kamer

Even as shape became soft instead of rigid
in the early years of the twentieth
century, its recourse was back to the
eighteenth century, finding its natural
counterpart in the détente of the 1780s
and 1790s. The elongated cylinder that
was replacing the hard and hyperbolic
body of the 1890s was recapitulating the
paradigm of fashion change that
happened from the 1770s to the 1790s.

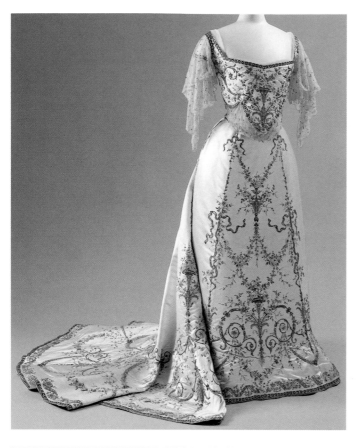

Jean-Philippe Worth. *Ball gown,* **front view and two details, 1900-1905**

Ice-blue silk satin embroidered in scrolling floral motif, lace, rhinestones. Gift of Mrs. Walter H. Page, 1979 (1979.251.4a,b)

With the fin-de-siècle and turn into the twentieth century, some changes were less clear-cut and decisive than the Dynamo and the Virgin. The House of Worth, where couture has been reified in the nineteenth century, became that time's conservative bastion at the beginning of the twentieth century. A taste for the eighteenth century was a trait of some contemporary moderns, from poet Charles Baudelaire to writer Marcel Proust, but the House of Worth took its eighteenth century literally and as a retreat from the modern in both silhouette and surface decoration. Within a decade or two, the House of Worth would be superannuated.

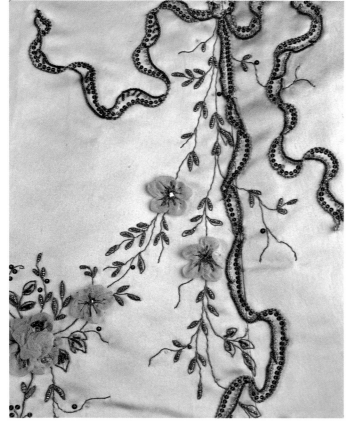

Christian Dior. *"Eventail"*
Cocktail Dress, detail and front
view, fall-winter 1956
Midnight- and royal-blue floral-patterned
silk taffeta. Gift of Muriel Rand, 1963
(CI 63.36 a-c)

Christian Dior. *"Nuit d'Août"*
ball gown, side view, spring-
summer 1954
White silk chiffon printed with yellow-rose
and green-leaf clusters. Gift of Mrs. Byron C.
Foy, 1956 (CI 56.60.5 a-d)

In his romantic "Aimant" collection,
Dior offered the emphatic reiteration of
his commitment to the eighteenth
century made modern. Here referring to
the ubiquitous fans women used to
"communicate" at court, Dior raised the
waist but delighted in the fullness of the
skirt and pronounced form of the bust. It
was, of course, the rigidity of inner
structure emanating from the corset that
permitted Dior the license of the strapless
gown, just as the décolletage of the
eighteenth century was made possible by
the shaping of the waist below and the
platform of bust support.

In this ball gown, Dior tendered one of
his most apparent evocations of the
eighteenth century in chiffon. While he
actually used an unbroken length of
chiffon tucked into the waist at the back
and separating into two trains, he seems
to have added an overdress to a petticoat
and then taken the swags of the
overdress into the form of an eighteenth-
century polonaise. One sign of Dior's
confidence in emulating the ancien
régime is that he did not hesitate to vary
the actual structure, inventing his own
means to resemble the effects of the
eighteenth century.

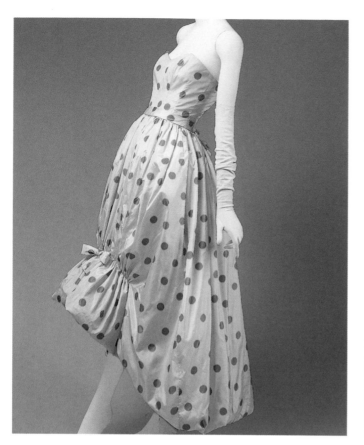

Cristobal Balenciaga. *Ball gown,*
side view, ca. 1956
*White taffeta with pink polka dots and pink
silk satin. Courtesy Martin Kamer*

In the 1950s, Balenciaga created grandiose
silhouettes using the suspension, drape, and
swagger of panniers, polonaises, and swags in
taffeta and satin. Balenciaga archivist Marie-
Andrée Jouve has perspicaciously compared
the effects of the swags to characteristics of
two Spanish painters: the animated drapery of
Zurbarán (1598-1664) and, to a lesser degree,
the emphatic shapes of Goya (1746-1828). In
this example, Balenciaga's chief affinity is to
the eighteenth century, though it must be
admitted that he probably preferred the
seventeenth century and the Second Empire
as fashion inspirations. Further, Balenciaga
tended to choose Spanish examples that
differentiate him considerably from the
parochial French nationalism of Dior. In fact,
Balenciaga favored Goya over eighteenth-
century French painters such as Fragonard or
Boucher.

Jeanne Lanvin. *Robe de Style,*
side view, 1922
*Blue silk faille trimmed with gold metallic
ribbon and embroidered with pearls and glass
beads. Gift of Mrs. Stephen C. Clark, 1962
(CI 62.8.5)*

Lanvin possessed one of the most cultured
imaginations in early twentieth-century
design. She studied Far Eastern and
Middle Eastern dress and textiles; she
understood and led the exploration for
avant-garde cylindrical design; and she
never forgot the panniered silhouette of
the eighteenth century that became the
robe de style. Lanvin was an historicist,
limiting the dilation of the hips to the
sides of her creations and maintaining a
flat broadened front and back, thus
establishing dress on the plane. That
two-dimensional plane was irresistible for
another Lanvin specialty: embroidery.

Christian Lacroix. *Evening
Ensemble,* front view,
fall-winter 1987

*Black synthetic faille, lace, dotted net,
and ribbon appliqué. Gift of Mrs. William
McCormick Blair, Jr., 1989
(1989.334.1a-e)*

Christian Lacroix. *Evening
ensemble,* back view, 1987

*Polychrome silk damask. Gift of Monika
Dorsey in memory of Hebe Dorsey, 1988
(1988.34.2a-c)*

By the time of Lacroix's "pouf," the style
had been so ardently revived in the
1860s and 1880s that many found it
difficult to recognize the original
eighteenth-century style. In fact, that
process of historical accretion was in
effect: a broad, supported skirt could
seem to manifest the Scarlett O'Hara
1860s, and the flared skirt and corseted
body could seem so innately belle
époque that one needed to look no
further or more deeply into history.
Visual and intellectual history have
sometimes obscured the eighteenth
century because of its almost inescapable
immanence.

Lacroix's "pouf," incipient in his work at
Jean Patou and canonized in his first
collection under his own name, is
recognizable by a massing and dilation of
the hips akin to the pannier. That this
style of the eighteenth-century court was
so vividly restored and so popular just
before an economic downturn seemed to
be judged in the later 1980s as an
aristocratic and courtly pretension that
was almost immediately deflated—
literally and figuratively—by Black
Monday, 1987. Lacroix's training as an art
historian has provided him with an
ability for many historical and aesthetic
references and refinements of his
sensibility that is gladly and
imperturbably joyous and buoyant.

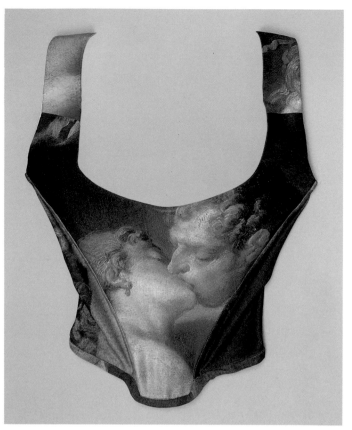

Boué Soeurs. *Court presentation dress and train,* front view, 1928
Pale-pink silk tulle and chiffon with metallic embroidery and silk polychrome flower appliqués. Gift of Mrs. George Henry O'Neil, 1968 (CI 68.48.a,b)

The robe de style silhouette, with its structural panniers augmenting the sides, is rendered by the Boué Soeurs as a light, flickering system of sheer, partially see-through layers rather than the hard carapace of eighteenth-century dresses. Whereas petticoats and inner structures of eighteenth-century clothing were solid and more or less rigid, the Boué Soeurs dress, despite the resemblance in silhouette, reveals its twentieth-century disposition in its lingerie-like revealing lightness, like the merest trellis for an arbor of silk flowers. A penchant for sweet, three-dimensional buds is, of course, shared by the rococo and the Boué Soeurs.

Vivienne Westwood. *Bodice,* front view, spring-summer 1994
Synthetic jersey printed with images from François Boucher's Hercules and Omphale. Gift of Richard Martin, 1994 (1994.465)

Paladin of a sweet and felicitous rococo, Boucher (1703-1770) is an apt artist for Westwood's claim to a romantic bodice. In portraiture and genre painting, Boucher captured the "sweet disarray" of eighteenth-century dress, whereas the painter's mythical maidens and nymphs were more often bare-breasted. But there is also an unmistakable crudeness and modernity to this creation, with its crassly printed image, almost more like a T-shirt graphic than one suitable for a bodice. The paradox of Westwood's almost-too-earnest historicism is that it is often rendered in poor quality. Is this Andy Warhol's *Thirty Are Better Than One,* comprised of thirty poor copies of the *Mona Lisa?* Or is this an advocacy of the eighteenth-century bodice, yet lacking its craft?

Vivienne Westwood. *Man's "pirate" ensemble (shirt and trousers),* **front view, 1981**
Black, gray, and plum striped cotton. Gift of Richard Martin, 1997 (1997.40.7 a,b)

The "pirate" collection marked Westwood's metamorphosis from contemporary culture and rock music as primary reference to history as fashion's critical implication. For that collection, Westwood studied men's shirts and trousers of the Tom Jones era for her swashbuckling and historicist pirate look. Ironically, Westwood retained her disestablishment edge in declaring them pirates, but the designer was inevitably declaring herself a scholar of costume history. Westwood was asked by *The Independent* (December 2, 1994) to reply to an eleven-year-old fan. She wrote, "First you must start to get a sense of beauty. Look at the paintings of many great masters; at Watteau, Boucher, and Fragonard. Look at Sèvres porcelain and French furniture and clocks, either in museums or in books from your nearest library."

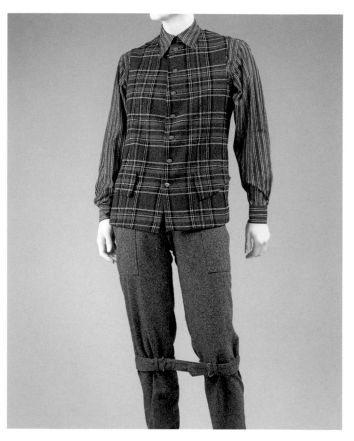

Vivienne Westwood. *Man's day ensemble (shirt, vest, trousers),* front view, fall-winter 1996-97
Burgundy and white striped cotton, polychrome plaid wool, and brown tweed wool. Gift of Richard Martin, 1997 (1997.40.2 a-c)

Persisting in her pursuit of the narrative implications of the eighteenth century, the matrix of the modern English novel, Westwood has continued to dress men in the style of that time, with her creation of elongated, collarless waistcoats and flamboyant shirts. In this case, Westwood slips back into early punk mode with bondage trousers, tethered at the knee, but this Hogarthian pilgrim is clearly less punk and more picaresque than the original version. Westwood has, of course, created many female counterparts, women who dress in the style of Moll Flanders.

Jean Paul Gaultier. *Man's coat,* back view, spring-summer 1994
Stone-washed denim. Gift of Richard Martin, 1994 (1994.467)

Like Westwood, Gaultier is an inveterate student of fashion history. His chronic turns to the eighteenth century are especially inflected by colonialism and globalism, often combining non-Western trousers and other effects with traditional signs of that period. But Gaultier carries his erudition perhaps more lightly than Westwood, insisting on such curious pastiches as the man's coat with flaring peplum that is from the silhouette of the eighteenth century but is rendered by Gaultier in the modern material of denim.

Left:

Jean Paul Gaultier. *Coat,* **back view, spring-summer 1994**
Pale-yellow cotton organdy with large shell buttons. Gift of Claudia Payne, 1996 (1996.482.6a)

Gaultier's faithful version of a man's coat (albeit transferred across genders) indicates the designer's interest in truth not only to representation of clothing but also to its actual construction. Gaultier knows the eighteenth century not only though prints and paintings but also through actual garment construction. But he does not make "fancy dress" or masquerade from such esoteric knowledge; his post-modern sensibility is always to transform, surrendering cognitive command of the past to an intuitive sensibility for the present. This coat has gone from male to female and from opaque to translucent material, two obvious signs of transfiguration.

Center:

English. *Man's Suit (coat, waistcoat, and breeches),* **front view, ca. 1760**
Purple wool with gilt-metal trim and buttons. Purchase, NAMSB Fund, 1996 (1996.117 a-c)

This exceptional mid-century wool suit, even in blue-purple, may seem relatively dour in comparison to the bright silks of much court dress. Before the Great Male Renunciation—a term defining the argument that men forsook color and decoration in apparel to partake of business, the Industrial Revolution, and sooty cities—men were still peacocks and paradigms of sartorial splendor. The eighteenth-century man will probably always stand as the most sartorially confident, consuming, and concupiscent man in history.

Right:

Jean Paul Gaultier. *Coat,* **side view, spring-summer 1994**
Blue silk/linen chambray with large self-fabric covered buttons. Gift of Richard Martin, 1994 (1994.576.3)

That menswear has become so conventional in the twentieth century has allowed its historical aberrations to stand out. In opposition to the canonical man's suit, the frock coat is long, elegant, and unabashedly anachronistic. Gaultier takes anachronistic menswear to be an option of reinterpretation as womenswear (and similar menswear, for example, p. 76). History plays a role in the process of displacement: historic distance enables an item of apparel, perhaps because the issues of power are academic, to shift more readily between menswear and womenswear. Gaultier devotes great attention to details: sleeve buttons actually work, and the side-pocket buttons here, as in the coat on the left on this page, are set low to allow the jacket to hike up slightly when buttoned.

ACKNOWLEDGMENTS

Benjamin Franklin, one of the geniuses of the eighteenth century whom we remember frequently for his wisdom and maxims that endure into the twentieth century, reported in his *Autobiography* that "Human felicity is produced not so much by great pieces of good fortune that seldom happen, as by little advantages that occur every day." So much of the felicity of this exhibition and book resides in the generous and everyday advantages of colleagues and the cooperation offered by others. In immediacy and in generosity, my associates and friends in The Costume Institute have contributed enormously to *The Ceaseless Century*: Liegh Acosta, Janie Butler, Anne Byrd, Deirdre Donohue, Michael Downer, Minda Drazin, Lisa Faibish, Ellen Fisher, Laura Foos, Rochelle Friedman, Dorothy Hanenberg, Stéphane Houy-Towner, Alexandra Kowalski, Wade Laboissonniere, Marilyn Lawrence, Becky Mark, Emily Martin, Kirsten Olsen, Bonnie Rosenblum, Birdie Schklowsky, Dennita Sewell, Rose Simon, and Judith Sommer. That eighteenth-century garments can mingle in this exhibition with those of our time is the triumph of Chris Paulocik's respectful and animating conservation and Jennifer Kibel's skills and subtlety in dressing and presentation. Karin Willis contributes her sharp eye to this process to render dress analytically and beautifully.

John P. O'Neill, Takaaki Matsumoto, and Barbara Cavaliere have helped me in every way with this book. From initial advocacy to final press review, John O'Neill has been an eighteenth-century gentleman and a good friend. I am grateful to Takaaki Matsumoto who has taken an *encyclopédie* of images and rendered them with clarity and elegance as a book. Barbara Cavaliere is, as always, friend and editor in roles we have rotated and refined for more than twenty years. I take privilege from working with these talented book people.

For the exhibition, I am especially grateful for the cooperation of Chanel, Stella McCartney for Chloe, Christian Lacroix, Paul Smith, Olivier Theyskens, and Patrizia Cucco of Gianni Versace. Janet Ozzard of the Paris bureau of *Women's Wear Daily* was most helpful. Martin Kamer, Titi Halle, and Cora Ginsburg aided with objects and ardor. Elsewhere in The Metropolitan Museum of Art, Richard Morsches, Linda Sylling, Barbara Weinberg, Michael Langley, Barbara Weiss, Zack Zanolli, Anna Marie Kellen, Harold Holzer, and Phylis Fogelson provided splendid service and support. Of Philippe de Montebello, we might pretend that we had two different exhibitions in mind, but one always knows that Philippe gives his unequivocal, whole-hearted confidence to the best exhibition possible.

I am not someone who has to be urged to interpretation, but I am inspired to offer as many ideas and options as possible by my friends Barbara Brickman, Nancy DuPuy, Eileen Ekstract, Julie Duer, Susan Furlaud, Betsy Kallop, Susan Lauren, Butzi Moffit, Victoria Munroe, Wendy Nolan, Pat Peterson, Christine Petschek, Dee Schaeffer, Nancy Silbert, and D. J. White. I learn from them.

The Ceaseless Century reminds us of our capacity and our yearning to learn from the past. Other than an example or two of "fancy dress" or "masquerade," the process is not copying but is instead a creative junction between contemporary expression and history. On the cusp of being modern, but always remaining pre-modern, the eighteenth century continues to provide us with an alternative to obdurate modernism. This is neither sterile and academic historicism nor the flamboyant masquerade of some who feign to make modern fashion; *The Ceaseless Century* is the flickering trace of being modern and retaining an evocative magic and a majesty in dress.

Richard Martin
Curator, The Costume Institute,
The Metropolitan Museum of Art

Baines, Barbara. *Fashion Revivals from the Elizabethan Age to the Present Day.* London: Batsford Books, 1981.

Buck, Anne. *Dress in Eighteenth-Century England.* New York: Holmes & Meier. 1979.

Culler, Dwight. *The Victorian Mirror of History.* New Haven: Yale University Press, 1985.

Cunnington, C. Willett and Phillis. *Handbook of English Costume in the Eighteenth Century.* London: Faber & Faber Ltd., 1954.

Fraser, Kennedy. *The Fashionable Mind: Reflections on Fashion, 1970-1981.* New York: Alfred A. Knopf, 1981.

Kidwell, Claudia Brush. "Are Those Clothes Real? Transforming the Way Eighteenth-Century Portraits are Studied," *Dress* 24, 1997, pp. 3-15.

Lipovetsky, Gilles. *The Empire of Fashion: Dressing Modern Democracy.* Princeton: Princeton University Press, 1994.

Martin, Richard. *Gianni Versace.* New York: The Metropolitan Museum of Art, 1997.

Martin, Richard and Harold Koda. *The Historical Mode: Fashion and Art in the 1980s.* New York: Rizzoli International Publications, 1989.

Ribeiro, Aileen. *The Art of Dress: Fashion in England and France, 1750 to 1820.* New Haven: Yale University Press, 1995.

—- *Dress in Eighteenth-Century Europe, 1715-1789.* New York: Holmes & Meier, 1985.

—- *Fashion in the French Revolution.* London: B. T. Batsford, 1988.

Roche, Daniel. *The Culture of Clothing: Dress and Fashion in the Ancien Régime.* Cambridge: Cambridge University Press, 1994.

—- *The People of Paris: An Essay in Popular Culture in the 18th Century.* New York: Berg Publishers, 1987.

SELECTED BIBLIOGRAPHY